HEALING TODAY

**Healing Scriptures and Confessions
for Every Day**

**Written and Arranged by
Pastor Al Gee**

Copyright © 2020
Durham, NC

Book Project Management—Start Write Publish
contact@startwriteaway.com
http://startwriteaway.com

<u>Start Write Team</u>
Editor: Dr. Gerald C. Simmons
Front/Back Cover/Book Illustration: Rainah Davis
Layout Design: Inkcept Studio

All bible quotes are from KJV and NIV unless otherwise stated.

All rights reserved.
No part of this publication may be reproduced, distributed, or transmitted in any form or by any means, including photocopying, recording, or other electronic or mechanical methods, without the prior written permission of the publisher, except in the case of brief quotations embodied in critical reviews and certain other noncommercial uses permitted by copyright law.

ISBN: 978-0-9994626-3-8

CONTENTS

Instructions: How We Fight 5

10 Important Statements on Divine Healing 7

30 Healing Miracles in the Bible 11

Healing Scriptures from the Old Testament 47

Healing Scriptures from the New Testament 57

Healing through Communion 73

INSTRUCTIONS

How We Fight

Some healing manifests as hands are laid immediately, and the prayer of faith is prayed. On the other hand, more often, there are times when healing does not manifest right away. Or, what is even more disturbing is that after an individual experiences a healing miracle, the infirmity later returns. This recurrence is absolutely not the time to doubt, but to fight the good "fight of faith!" All the promises of God are sure, but since we have an enemy determined through doubt to rob us of our right to be healed, we must fight to receive it. On the other hand, following a strict spiritual and physical regimen can serve as a powerful means of achieving and maintaining wellness in the above vital areas.

1. Obey the principles of proper nutrition and physical exercise.
2. At least three times a day, open your Bible and literally feed on healing Word. Meditate on healing scriptures day and night. YOU MUST SEE YOURSELF AS THE WORD SAYS… "HEALED."
3. Treat sickness the same as we treat sin. We don't deny its existence, but we deny its right to stay in our bodies.
4. Take communion often, claiming your blood covenant right to be healed, saying, "My sins are all forgiven. My body is legally released from all diseases" (Isa. 53:4-5 KJV).
5. Plant the Word like a seed into your spirit by reading and speaking it. Then, expect the harvest of healing in your body. YOU REAP WHATEVER YOU SOW! (Mk 4:26-29; Gal. 6:7).
6. DO NOT FEAR, AND DO NOT WORRY (Phil. 4:6; 2 Tim. 1:7).
7. Don't take "No" for an answer.

10 IMPORTANT STATEMENTS ON DIVINE HEALING

1. Sickness comes from the enemy. It is the foul offspring of its father, Satan and its mother, sin. It is part of the curse and the oppression of the enemy (Deut. 28: 15-68; Acts 10:38).

2. Sickness came into the world through the sin of man. By Adam's sin, death entered our world. Sickness is a primary cause of death. Its true remedy is the blood atonement of Christ (Rom. 5:12; 1 Peter 2:24).

3. Divine healing is an essential part of our salvation and the Gospel. It is an essential part of our Covenant with God (Exod. 23:25; Mark 16:18).

4. Uncertainty as to whether it's God's will to heal or not is a significant obstacle to being healed. Praying, "if it be thy will," is not a strong faith stand regarding healing (Mark 1:40-41).

5. Divine healing is not automatic. Just as Israel had to fight fearsome giants for the land God promised, we also must fight the fight of faith against terrible diseases for the healing God promises us (1 Tim. 6:12).

6. The Word of God is as powerful as seeds for healing. The baptized believer can plant them and expect results, just as the farmer who plants his seeds expecting a harvest. We are assured, "we shall reap if we don't give up" (Gal. 6:7-9).

7. Healing by God's Word is by the Spirit into the body. God's Word must be believed and acted upon to gain the results. (Prov. 4:20-22)

8. There are two reports one is from the senses or the physical, and the other one is from the Word of God or the spiritual. (Isa. 53:1; 2 Cor. 4:18)
9. At the cross, not only were our sins forgiven, but our sicknesses were also carried away (Psalms 103:3; Isa. 53:4-5).
10. With the same determination that we resist sin, we should also resist sickness.

30 HEALING MIRACLES IN THE BIBLE

MIRACLE #1: NOBLEMAN'S SON

JOHN 4:46-54
Jesus Heals Young Boy

46 Once more he visited Cana in Galilee, where he had turned the water into wine. And there was a certain royal official whose son lay sick at Capernaum. 47 When this man heard that Jesus had arrived in Galilee from Judea, he went to him and begged him to come and heal his son, who was close to death. 48 "Unless you people see signs and wonders," Jesus told him, "you will never believe." 49 The royal official said, "Sir, come down before my child dies."

50 "Go," Jesus replied, "your son will live." The man took Jesus at his word and departed.

51 While he was still on the way, his servants met him with the news that his boy was living.

52 When he inquired as to the time when his son got better, they said to him, "Yesterday, at one in the afternoon, the fever left him."53 Then the father realized that this was the exact time at which Jesus had said to him, "Your son will live." So he and his whole household believed.

54 This was the second sign Jesus performed after coming from Judea to Galilee.

MIRACLE #2:
PETER'S WIFE'S MOTHER

LUKE 4:38-39
Jesus Heals Woman with Fever

38 Jesus left the synagogue and went to the home of Simon. Now Simon's mother-in-law was suffering from a high fever, and they asked Jesus to help her.

39 So he bent over her and rebuked the fever, and it left her. She got up at once and began to wait on them.

MIRACLE #3:
HE HEALED THEM ALL

MATTHEW 14:34-36
Jesus Healed All that Were Diseased

34 When they had crossed over, they landed at Gennesaret. 35 And when the men of that place recognized Jesus, they sent word to all the surrounding country. People brought all their sick to him. 36 and begged him to let the sick just touch the edge of his cloak, and all who touched it were healed.

MIRACLE #4:
A LEPER

MARK 1:40-45
Jesus Heals a Man with Leprosy

40 A man with leprosy came to him and begged him on his knees, "If you are willing, you can make me clean." 41 Jesus was indignant. He reached out his hand and touched the man. "I am willing," he said. "Be clean!" 42 Immediately the leprosy left him, and he was cleansed

43 Jesus sent him away at once with a strong warning: 44 "See that you don't tell this to anyone. But go, show yourself to the priest and offer the sacrifices that Moses commanded for your cleansing, as a testimony to them." 45 Instead, he went out and began to talk freely, spreading the news. As a result, Jesus could no longer enter a town openly but stayed outside in lonely places. Yet the people still came to him from everywhere.

MIRACLE #5: A PARALYTIC MAN

MATTHEW 9:1-8
Jesus Forgives and Heals a Paralyzed Man

1 Jesus stepped into a boat, crossed over, and came to his own town. 2 Some men brought to him a paralyzed man lying on a mat. When Jesus saw their faith, he said to the man, "Take heart, son; your sins are forgiven." 3 At this, some of the teachers of the law said to themselves, "This fellow is blaspheming!" 4 Knowing their thoughts,

Jesus said, "Why do you entertain evil thoughts in your hearts? 5 Which is easier: to say, 'Your sins are forgiven,' or to say, 'Get up and walk'? 6 But I want you to know that the Son of Man has authority on earth to forgive sins." So he said to the paralyzed man, "Get up, take your mat and go home." 7 Then the man got up and went home. 8 When the crowd saw this, they were filled with awe; and they praised God, who had given such authority to man.

MIRACLE #6: MAN AT THE POOL

JOHN 5:2-15
Jesus Heals Man at the Pool

2 Now there is in Jerusalem near the Sheep Gate a pool, which in Aramaic is called Bethesda and which is surrounded by five covered colonnades. 3 Here a great number of disabled people used to lie— the blind, the lame, the paralyzed—and they waited for the moving of the waters.

4 From time to time, an angel of the Lord would come down and stir up the waters. The first one into the pool after each such disturbance would be cured of whatever disease they had. 5 One who was there had been an invalid for thirty-eight years. 6 When Jesus saw him lying there and learned that he had been in this condition for a long time, he asked him, "Do you want to get well?" 7 "Sir," the invalid replied, "I have no one to help me into the pool when the water is stirred. While I am trying to get in, someone else goes down ahead of me." 8 Then Jesus said to him, "Get up! Pick up your mat and walk." 9 At once, the man was cured; he picked up his mat and walked. The day on which this took place was a Sabbath, 10 and so the Jewish leaders said to the man who had been healed, "It is the Sabbath; the law forbids you to carry your mat."

11 But he replied, "The man who made me well said to me, 'Pick up your mat and walk.'"

12 So they asked him, "Who is this fellow who told you to pick it up and walk?" 13

The man who was healed had no idea who it was, for Jesus had slipped away into the crowd that was there.

14 Later Jesus found him at the temple and said to him, "See, you are well again. Stop sinning, or something worse may happen to you." 15 The man went away and told the Jewish leaders that it was Jesus who had made him well.

MIRACLE #7:
MAN WITH THE WITHERED HAND

MATTHEW 12:9-13
Jesus Heals the Withered Hand of a Man

9 Going on from that place, he went into their synagogue, 10 and a man with a shriveled hand was there. Looking for a reason to bring charges against Jesus, they asked him, "Is it lawful to heal on the Sabbath?" 11 He said to them, "If any of you has a sheep and it falls into a pit on the Sabbath, will you not take hold of it and lift it out?

12 How much more valuable is a person than a sheep! Therefore it is lawful to do good on the Sabbath." 13 Then he said to the man, "Stretch out your hand." So he stretched it out, and it was completely restored, just as sound as the other.

MIRACLE #8: THE CENTURION'S SERVANT

MATTHEW 8:5-13
The Faith of the Centurion

5 When Jesus had entered Capernaum, a centurion came to him, asking for help. 6 "Lord," he said, "my servant lies at home paralyzed, suffering terribly." 7 Jesus said to him, "Shall I come and heal him?" 8 The centurion replied, "Lord, I do not deserve to have you come under my roof. But just say the word, and my servant will be healed. 9 For I myself am a man under authority, with soldiers under me. I tell this one, 'Go,' and he goes; and that one, 'Come,' and he comes. I say to my servant, 'Do this,' and he does it." 10 When Jesus heard this, he was amazed and said to those following him, "Truly I tell you, I have not found anyone in Israel with such great faith. 11 I say to you that many will come from the east and the west, and will take their places at the feast with Abraham, Isaac, and Jacob in the kingdom of heaven.

12 But the subjects of the kingdom will be thrown outside, into the darkness, where there will be weeping and gnashing of teeth." 13 Then Jesus said to the centurion, "Go! Let it be done just as you believed it would." And his servant was healed at that moment.

MIRACLE #9: JAIRUS' DAUGHTER

MATTHEW 9:18-26
Jesus Raises a Dead Girl and Heals a Sick Woman

18 While he was saying this, a synagogue leader came and knelt before him and said, "My daughter has just died. But come and put your hand on her, and she will live." 19 Jesus got up and went with him, and so did his disciples. 20 Just then, a woman who had been subject to bleeding for twelve years came up behind him and touched the edge of his cloak. 21 She said to herself, "If I only touch his cloak, I will be healed." 22 Jesus turned and saw her. "Take heart, daughter," he said, "your faith has healed you." And the woman was healed at that moment.

23 When Jesus entered the synagogue leader's house and saw the noisy crowd and people playing pipes, 24 he said, "Go away. The girl is not dead but asleep." But they laughed at him.

25 After the crowd had been put outside, he went in and took the girl by the hand, and she got up. 26 News of this spread through all that region.

MIRACLE #10:
THE WOMAN WITH ISSUE OF BLOOD

MARK 5:25-34
Jesus' Anointing Heals Woman with Issue of Blood

25 And a woman was there who had been subject to bleeding for twelve years. 26 She had suffered a great deal under the care of many doctors and had spent all she had, yet instead of getting better she grew worse. 27 When she heard about Jesus, she came up behind him in the crowd and touched his cloak, 28 because she thought, "If I just touch his clothes, I will be healed." 29 Immediately her bleeding stopped, and she felt in her body that she was freed from her suffering. 30 At once, Jesus realized that power had gone out from him. He turned around in the crowd and asked, "Who touched my clothes?" 31 "You see the people crowding against you," his disciples answered, "and yet you can ask, 'Who touched me?' " 32 But Jesus kept looking around to see who had done it. 33 Then the woman, knowing what had happened to her, came and fell at his feet and, trembling with fear, told him the whole truth. 34 He said to her, "Daughter, your faith has healed you. Go in peace and be freed from your suffering."

MIRACLE #11:
TWO BLIND MEN

MATTHEW 9:27-31
Jesus Heals the Blind and the Mute

27 As Jesus went on from there, two blind men followed him, calling out, "Have mercy on us, Son of David!" 28 When he had gone indoors, the blind men came to him, and he asked them, "Do you believe that I am able to do this?" "Yes, Lord," they replied. 29 Then he touched their eyes and said, "According to your faith let it be done to you;" 30, and their sight was restored. Jesus warned them sternly, "See that no one knows about this." 31 But they went out and spread the news about him all over that region.

MIRACLE #12:
THE SYROPHOENICIAN'S DAUGHTER

MATTHEW 15:21-28
The Faith of a Canaanite Woman

21 Leaving that place, Jesus withdrew to the region of Tyre and Sidon. 22 A

Canaanite woman from that vicinity came to him, crying out, "Lord, Son of David, have mercy on me! My daughter is demon-possessed and suffering terribly." 23 Jesus did not answer a word. So his disciples came to him and urged him, "Send her away, for she keeps crying out after us." 24 He answered, "I was sent only to the lost sheep of Israel." 25 The woman came and knelt before him. "Lord, help me!" she said. 26 He replied, "It is not right to take the children's bread and toss it to the dogs." 27 "Yes, it is, Lord," she said. "Even the dogs eat the crumbs that fall from their master's table." 28 Then Jesus said to her, "Woman, you have great faith! Your request is granted." And her daughter was healed at that moment.

MIRACLE #13:
THE DEAF MAN WITH SPEECH IMPEDIMENT

MARK 7:31-37
Jesus Heals a Deaf and Mute Man

31 Then Jesus left the vicinity of Tyre and went through Sidon, down to the Sea of

Galilee and into the region of the Decapolis. 32 There some people brought to him a man who was deaf and could hardly talk, and they begged Jesus to place his hand on him. 33 After he took him aside, away from the crowd, Jesus put his fingers into the man's ears. Then he spit and touched the man's tongue. 34 He looked up to heaven and with a deep sigh said to him, "Ephphatha!" which means "Be opened!" 35 At this, the man's ears were opened, his tongue was loosened, and he began to speak plainly. 36 Jesus commanded them not to tell anyone. But the more he did so, the more they kept talking about it. 37 People were overwhelmed with amazement. "He has done everything well," they said. "He even makes the deaf hear, and the mute speak."

MIRACLE #14:
BLIND MAN AT BETHSAIDA

MARK 8:22-26
Jesus Heals a Blind Man at Bethsaida

22 They came to Bethsaida, and some people brought a blind man and begged

Jesus to touch him. 23 He took the blind man by the hand and led him outside the village. When he had spit on the man's eyes and put his hands on him, Jesus asked, "Do you see anything?" 24 He looked up and said, "I see people; they look like trees walking around." 25 Once more, Jesus put his hands on the man's eyes. Then his eyes were opened, his sight was restored, and he saw everything clearly. 26 Jesus sent him home, saying, "Don't even go into the village."

MIRACLE #15: LUNATIC SON

MARK 9:14-29
Jesus Heals a Boy Possessed by an Impure Spirit

14 When they came to the other disciples, they saw a large crowd around them and the teachers of the law arguing with them. 15 As soon as all the people saw Jesus, they were overwhelmed with wonder and ran to greet him. 16 "What are you arguing with them about?" he asked. 17 A man in the crowd answered, "Teacher, I brought you my son, who is possessed by a spirit that has robbed him of speech. 18 Whenever it seizes him, it throws him to the ground. He foams at the mouth, gnashes his teeth, and becomes rigid. I asked your disciples to drive out the spirit, but they could not." 19 "You unbelieving generation," Jesus replied, "how long shall I stay with you? How long shall I put up with you? Bring the boy to me." 20 So they brought him. When the spirit saw Jesus, it immediately threw the boy into a convulsion. He fell to the ground and rolled around, foaming at the mouth. 21 Jesus asked the boy's father, "How long has he been like this?" From childhood," he answered. 22 "It has often thrown him into fire or water to kill him. But if you can do anything, take pity on us and help us." 23 "'If you can'?" said Jesus. "Everything is possible for one who believes." 24 Immediately the boy's father exclaimed, "I do believe; 25 When Jesus saw that a crowd was running to the scene, he rebuked the impure spirit. "You deaf and mute spirit," he said, "I command you, come out of him and never enter him again." 26 The spirit shrieked, convulsed him violently, and came out. The boy looked so much like a corpse that many said, "He's dead." 27 But Jesus took him by the hand and lifted him to his feet, and he stood up. 28 After Jesus had gone indoors, his disciples asked him privately, "Why couldn't we drive it out?" 29 He replied, "This kind can come out only by prayer and fasting."

MIRACLE #16 : MAN BORN BLIND

JOHN 9:1-7
Jesus Heals a Man Born Blind

1 As he went along, he saw a man blind from birth. 2 His disciples asked him, "Rabbi, who sinned, this man or his parents, that he was born blind?" 3 "Neither this man nor his parents sinned," said Jesus, "but this happened so that the works of God might be displayed in him. 4 As long as it is day, we must do the works of him who sent me. Night is coming, when no one can work. 5 While I am in the world, I am the light of the world." 6 After saying this, he spit on the ground, made some mud with the saliva, and put it on the man's eyes. 7 "Go," he told him, "wash in the Pool of Siloam" (this word means "Sent"). So the man went and washed, and came home seeing.

MIRACLE #17:
WOMAN WITH THE SPIRIT OF INFIRMITY

LUKE 13:10-17
Jesus Heals a Crippled Woman on the Sabbath

10 On a Sabbath, Jesus was teaching in one of the synagogues, 11 and a woman was there who had been crippled by a spirit for eighteen years. She was bent over and could not straighten up at all. 12 When Jesus saw her, he called her forward and said to her, "Woman, you are set free from your infirmity." 13 Then he put his hands on her, and immediately she straightened up and praised God. 14 Indignant because Jesus had healed on the Sabbath, the synagogue leader said to the people, "There are six days for work. So come and be healed on those days, not on the Sabbath." 15 The Lord answered him, "You hypocrites! Doesn't each of you on the Sabbath untie your ox or donkey from the stall and lead it out to give it water? 16 Then should not this woman, a daughter of Abraham, whom Satan has kept bound for eighteen long years, be set free on the Sabbath day from what bound her?" 17 When he said this, all his opponents were humiliated, but the people were delighted with all the wonderful things he was doing.

MIRACLE #18:
MAN WITH DROPSY

LUKE 14:1-6
Jesus at a Pharisee's House

1 One Sabbath, when Jesus went to eat in the house of a prominent Pharisee, he was being carefully watched. 2 There in front of him was a man suffering from abnormal swelling of his body. 3 Jesus asked the

Pharisees and experts in the law, "Is it lawful to heal on the Sabbath or not?" 4 But they remained silent. So taking hold of the man, he healed him and sent him on his way. 5 Then he asked them, "If one of you has a child or an ox that falls into a well on the Sabbath day, will you not immediately pull it out?" 6 And they had nothing to say.

MIRACLE #19: TEN LEPERS

LUKE 17:11-19
Jesus Heals Ten Men with Leprosy

11 Now on his way to Jerusalem, Jesus traveled along the border between Samaria and Galilee. 12 As he was going into a village, ten men who had leprosy met him. They stood at a distance 13 and called out in a loud voice, "Jesus, Master, have pity on us!" 14 When he saw them, he said, "Go, show yourselves to the priests." And as they went, they were cleansed. 15 One of them, when he saw he was healed, came back, praising God in a loud voice. 16 He threw himself at Jesus' feet and thanked him—and he was a Samaritan. 17 Jesus asked, "Were not all ten cleansed? Where are the other nine? 18 Has no one returned to give praise to God except this foreigner?" 19 Then he said to him, "Rise and go; your faith has made you well."

MIRACLE #20: JESUS HEALS THE SICK

MATTHEW 4:23-25
Large Crowds Healed

23 Jesus went throughout Galilee, teaching in their synagogues, proclaiming the good news of the kingdom, and healing every disease and sickness among the people. 24 News about him spread all over Syria, and people brought to him all who were ill with various diseases, those suffering severe pain, the demon-possessed, those having seizures, and the paralyzed; and He healed them. 25 Large crowds from Galilee, the Decapolis, Jerusalem, Judea, and the region across the Jordan followed him.

MIRACLE #21:
BLIND AND MUTE DEMONIAC

MATTHEW 12:22-23
Jesus Heals Demon-Possessed Man

22 Then they brought him a demon-possessed man who was blind and mute, and Jesus healed him so that he could both talk and see. 23 All the people were astonished and said, "Could this be the Son of David?"

MIRACLE #22:
WIDOW'S SON RAISED

LUKE 7:12-15
Jesus Heals Widow's Son

12 As he approached the town gate, a dead person was being carried out—the only son of his mother, and she was a widow. And a large crowd from the town was with her. 13 When the Lord saw her, his heart went out to her, and he said, "Don't cry." 14 Then he went up and touched the bier they were carrying him on, and the bearers stood still. He said,

"Young man, I say to you, get up!" 15 Tne dead man sat up and began to talk, and Jesus gave him back to his mother.

MIRACLE #23: MALCHUS' EAR

LUKE 22:50-51
Jesus Touches and Heals a Man's Ear

50 And one of them struck the servant of the high priest, cutting off his right ear. 51 But Jesus answered, "No more of this!" And he touched the man's ear and healed him.

MIRACLE #24: LAZARUS

JOHN 11:1-44
Jesus Raises Lazarus from the Dead

The Death of Lazarus

1 Now a man named Lazarus was sick. He was from Bethany, the village of Mary and her sister Martha. 2 (This Mary, whose brother Lazarus now lay sick, was the same one who poured perfume on the Lord and wiped his feet with her hair.) 3 So the sisters sent word to Jesus, "Lord, the one you love is sick." 4 When he heard this, Jesus said, "This sickness will not end in death. No, it is for God's glory so that God's Son may be glorified through it." 5 Now Jesus loved Martha and her sister and Lazarus. 6 So when he heard that Lazarus was sick, he stayed where he was two more days,7 and then he said to his disciples, "Let us go back to Judea."

8 "But Rabbi," they said, "a short while ago the Jews there tried to stone you, and yet you are going back?"

9 Jesus answered, "Are there not twelve hours of daylight? Anyone who walks in the daytime will not stumble, for they see by this world's light. 10 It is when a person walks at night that they stumble, for they have no light." 11 After he had said this, he went on to tell them, "Our friend Lazarus has fallen asleep, but I am going there to wake him up." 12 His disciples replied, "Lord if he sleeps, he will get better." 13 Jesus had been speaking of his death, but his disciples thought he meant natural sleep. 14 So then he told them plainly, "Lazarus is dead, 15 and for your sake, I am glad I was not there, so that you may believe. But let us go to him." 16 Then Thomas (also known as Didymus) said to the rest of the disciples, "Let us also go, that we may die with him."

Jesus Comforts the Sisters of Lazarus

17 On his arrival, Jesus found that Lazarus had already been in the tomb for four days. 18 Now Bethany was less than two miles from Jerusalem, 19 and many Jews had come to Martha and Mary to comfort them in the loss of their brother. 20 When Martha heard that Jesus was coming, she went out to meet him, but Mary stayed at home. 21 "Lord," Martha said to Jesus, "if you had been here, my brother would not have died. 22 But I know that even now God will give you whatever you ask." 23 Jesus said to her, "Your brother will rise again." 24 Martha answered, "I know he will rise again in the resurrection at the last day." 25 Jesus said to her, "I am the resurrection and the life. The one who believes in me will live, even though they

die; 26 and whoever lives by believing in me will never die. Do you believe this?" 27 "Yes, Lord," she replied, "I believe that you are the Messiah, the Son of God, who is to come into the world." 28 After she had said this, she went back and called her sister Mary aside. "The Teacher is here," she said, "and is asking for you." 29 When Mary heard this, she got up quickly and went to him. 30 Now Jesus had not yet entered the village but was still at the place where Martha had met him. 31 When the Jews who had been with Mary in the house, comforting her, noticed how quickly she got up and went out, they followed her, supposing she was going to the tomb to mourn there. 32 When Mary reached the place where Jesus was and saw him, she fell at his feet and said, "Lord, if you had been here, my brother would not have died." 33 When Jesus saw her weeping, and the Jews who had come along with her also weeping, he was deeply moved in spirit and troubled. 34 "Where have you laid him?" he asked. "Come and see, Lord," they replied. 35 Jesus wept. 36 Then the Jews said, "See how he loved him!" 37 But some of them said, "Could not he who opened the eyes of the blind man have kept this man from dying?"

Jesus Raises Lazarus From the Dead

38 Jesus, once more deeply moved, came to the tomb. It was a cave with a stone laid across the entrance. 39 "Take away the stone," he said. "But, Lord," said Martha, the sister of the dead man, "by this time there is a bad odor, for he has been there four days." 40 Then Jesus said, "Did I not tell you that if you believe, you will see the glory of God?" 41 So they took away the stone. Then Jesus looked up and said, "Father, I thank you that you have heard me. 42 I knew that you always hear me, but I said this for the benefit of the people standing here, that they may believe that you sent me." 43 When he had said this, Jesus called in a loud voice, "Lazarus, come out!" 44 The dead man came out, his hands and feet wrapped with strips of linen and a cloth around his face. Jesus said to them, "Take off the grave clothes and let him go."

MIRACLE #25: PARALYTIC

MARK 2:1-12
Jesus Forgives and Heals a Paralyzed Man

1 A few days later, when Jesus again entered Capernaum, the people heard that he had come home. 2 They gathered in such large numbers that there was no room left, not even outside the door, and he preached the word to them. 3 Some men came, bringing to him a paralyzed man, carried by four of them. 4 Since they could not get him to Jesus because of the crowd, they made an opening in the roof above Jesus by digging through it and then lowered the mat the man was lying on. 5 When Jesus saw their faith, he said to the paralyzed man, "Son, your sins are forgiven." 6 Now some teachers of the law were sitting there, thinking to themselves, 7 "Why does this fellow talk like that? He's blaspheming! Who can forgive sins but God alone?"

8 Immediately Jesus knew in his spirit that this was what they were thinking in their hearts, and he said to them, "Why are you thinking these things? 9 Which is easier: to say to this paralyzed man, 'Your sins are forgiven,' or to say, 'Get up, take your mat and walk'? 10 But I want you to know that the Son of Man has authority on earth to forgive sins." So he said to the man, 11 "I tell you, get up, take your mat and go home." 12 He got up, took his mat, and walked out in full view of them all. This amazed everyone, and they praised God, saying, "We have never seen anything like this!"

MIRACLE #26:
MAN WITH THE WITHERED HAND

LUKE 6:6-10
Jesus Heals Man with Withered Hand

6 On another Sabbath, he went into the synagogue and was teaching, and a man was there whose right hand was shriveled. 7 The Pharisees and the teachers of the law were looking for a reason to accuse Jesus, so they watched him closely to see if he would heal on the Sabbath.

8 But Jesus knew what they were thinking and said to the man with the shriveled hand, "Get up and stand in front of everyone." So he got up and stood there. 9 Then Jesus said to them, "I ask you, which is lawful on the Sabbath: to do good or to do evil, to save life or to destroy it?"

10 He looked around at them all, and then said to the man, "Stretch out your hand." He did so, and his hand was completely restored.

MIRACLE #27:
PAUL HEALS THE SICK

ACTS 28:3-10
Paul Ashore on Malta

3 Paul gathered a pile of brushwood and, as he put it on the fire, a viper, driven out by the heat, fastened itself on his hand. 4 When the islanders saw the snake hanging from his hand, they said to each other, "This man must be a murderer; for though he escaped from the sea, the goddess Justice has not allowed him to live." 5 But Paul shook the snake off into the fire and suffered no ill effects. 6 The people expected him to swell up or suddenly fall dead, but after waiting a long time and seeing nothing unusual happen to him, they changed their minds and said he was a god. 7 There was an estate nearby that belonged to Publius, the chief official of the island. He welcomed us to his home and showed us generous hospitality for three days. 8 His father was sick in bed, suffering from fever and dysentery. Paul went in to see him and, after prayer, placed his hands on him and healed him. 9 When this had happened, the rest of the sick on the island came and were cured. 10 They honored us in many ways, and when we were ready to sail, they furnished us with the supplies we needed.

MIRACLE #28: LAME BEGGAR HEALED

ACTS 3:1-8
Peter Heals a Lame Beggar

1 One day Peter and John were going up to the temple at the time of prayer—at three in the afternoon. 2 Now a man who was lame from birth was being carried to the temple gate called Beautiful, where he was put every day to beg from those going into the temple courts. 3 When he saw Peter and John about to enter, he asked them for money. 4 Peter looked straight at him, as did John. Then Peter said, "Look at us!" 5 So the man gave them his attention, expecting to get something from them. 6 Then Peter said, "Silver or gold I do not have, but what I do have I give you. In the name of Jesus Christ of Nazareth, walk." 7 Taking him by the right hand, he helped him up, and instantly the man's feet and ankles became strong. 8 He jumped to his feet and began to walk. Then he went with them into the temple courts, walking and jumping and praising God.

MIRACLE #29: BLIND BARTIMAEUS

MARK 10:46-52
Blind Bartimaeus Receives His Sight

46 Then they came to Jericho. As Jesus and his disciples, together with a large crowd, were leaving the city, a blind man, Bartimaeus (which means "son of

Timaeus"), was sitting by the roadside begging. 47 When he heard that it was Jesus of Nazareth, he began to shout, "Jesus, Son of David, have mercy on me!" 48 Many rebuked him and told him to be quiet, but he shouted all the more, "Son of David, have mercy on me!" 49 Jesus stopped and said, "Call him." So they called to the blind man, "Cheer up! On your feet! He's calling you." 50 Throwing his cloak aside, he jumped to his feet and came to Jesus. 51 "What do you want me to do for you?" Jesus asked him. The blind man said, "Rabbi, I want to see." 52 "Go," said Jesus, "your faith has healed you." Immediately he received his sight and followed Jesus along the road.

MIRACLE #30:
ALL MANNER OF SICKNESS

MATTHEW 4:23-25
Jesus' Anointing Healed All Sickness & Diseases

23 Jesus went throughout Galilee, teaching in their synagogues, proclaiming the good news of the kingdom, and healing every

disease and sickness among the people. 24 News about him spread all over Syria, and people brought to him all who were ill with various diseases, those suffering severe pain, the demon-possessed, those having seizures, and the paralyzed; and he healed them. 25 Large crowds from Galilee, the Decapolis, Jerusalem, Judea, and the region across the Jordan followed him.

Dear Reader,

The word of God is seed. It is medicine and healing to every part of the body. To treat it like seed, it has to be planted in our hearts and minds. We have taken the liberty of going through the bible and finding every scripture that we could on healing.

Please use these scriptures as the farmer uses seed, expecting a harvest! We are admonished through scripture that if we want to be successful-we can't let his Word depart from our eyes or heart. We must meditate on it day and night.

Blessings, Pastor Al Gee

HEALING SCRIPTURES FROM THE OLD TESTAMENT

EXODUS

EXODUS 15:26

He said, "If you listen carefully to the Lord your God and do what is right in his eyes, if you pay attention to his commands and keep all his decrees, I will not bring on you any of the diseases I brought on the Egyptians, for I am the Lord, who heals you."

EXODUS 23:25

Worship the Lord your God, and his blessing will be on your food and water. I will take away sickness from among you

DEUTERONOMY

DEUTERONOMY 7:14-15

14 You will be blessed more than any other people; none of your men or women will be childless, nor will any of your livestock be without young.

15 The Lord will keep you free from every disease. He will not inflict on you the horrible diseases you knew in Egypt, but he will inflict them on all who hate you.

DEUTERONOMY 28:1-13

1 If you fully obey the Lord your God and carefully follow all his commands I give you today, the Lord your God will set you high above all the nations on earth.

2 All these blessings will come on you and accompany you if you obey the Lord your God

3 You will be blessed in the city and blessed in the country.

4 The fruit of your womb will be blessed, and the crops of your land and the young of your livestock—the calves of your herds and the lambs of your flocks.

5 Your basket and your kneading trough will be blessed.

6 You will be blessed when you come in and blessed when you go out.

7 The Lord will grant that the enemies who rise up against you will be defeated before you. They will come at you from one direction but flee from you in seven.

8 The Lord will send a blessing on your barns and on everything you put your hand to. The Lord your God will bless you in the land he is giving you.

9 The Lord will establish you as his holy people, as he promised you on oath, if you keep the commands of the Lord your God and walk in obedience to him.

10 Then all the peoples on earth will see that you are called by the name of the Lord, and they will fear you.

11 The Lord will grant you abundant prosperity—in the fruit of your womb, the young of your livestock and the crops of your ground—in the land he swore to your ancestors to give you.

12 The Lord will open the heavens, the storehouse of his bounty, to send rain on your land in season and to bless all the work of your hands. You will lend to many nations but will borrow from none.

13 The Lord will make you the head, not the tail. If you pay attention to the commands of the Lord your God that I give you this day and carefully follow them, you will always be at the top, never at the bottom.

DEUTERONOMY 30:19–20

19 This day I call the heavens and the earth as witnesses against you that I have set before you life and death, blessings and curses. Now choose life, so that you and your children may live

20 ...and that you may love the Lord your God, listen to his voice, and hold fast to him. For the Lord is your life, and he will give you many years in the land he swore to give to your fathers, Abraham, Isaac and Jacob.

1 KINGS

1 KINGS 8:56

Praise be to the Lord, who has given rest to his people Israel just as he promised. Not one word has failed of all the good promises he gave through his servant Moses.

PSALMS

PSALM 91:9-10

9 If you say, The Lord is my refuge, and you make the Most High your dwelling,

10 ...no harm will overtake you, no disaster will come near your tent.

PSALM 91:14-16

14 "Because he loves me," says the Lord, "I will rescue him; I will protect him, for he acknowledges my name.

15 He will call on me, and I will answer him; I will be with him in trouble, I will deliver him and honor him.

16 With long life I will satisfy him and show him my salvation."

PSALM 103:1-5

1 Praise the Lord, my soul; all my inmost being, praise his holy name.

2 Praise the Lord, my soul, and forget not all his benefits—

3 ...who forgives all your sins and heals all your diseases,

4 who redeems your life from the pit and crowns you with love and compassion,

5 who satisfies your desires with good things so that your youth is renewed like the eagles.

PSALM 107:8

Let them give thanks to the Lord for his unfailing love and his wonderful deeds for mankind...

PSALM 107:19-20

19 Then they cried to the Lord in their trouble, and he saved them from their distress.

20 He sent out his word and healed them; he rescued them from the grave.

PSALM 118:17

I will not die but live, and will proclaim what the Lord has done.

PROVERBS

PROVERBS 4:20-22

20 My son, pay attention to what I say; turn your ear to my words.

21 Do not let them out of your sight, keep them within your heart;

22 for they are life to those who find them and health to one's whole body.

ISAIAH

ISAIAH 40:28-31

28 Do you not know? Have you not heard? The Lord is the everlasting God, the Creator of the ends of the earth. He will not grow tired or weary, and his understanding no one can fathom.

29 He gives strength to the weary and increases the power of the weak.

30 Even youths grow tired and weary, and young men stumble and fall;

31 but those who hope in the Lord will renew their strength. They will soar on wings like eagles; they will run and not grow weary, they will walk and not be faint.

ISAIAH 41:10

So do not fear, for I am with you; do not be dismayed, for I am your God. I will strengthen you and help you; I will uphold you with my righteous right hand.

ISAIAH 53:4-5

4 Surely he took up our pain and bore our suffering, yet we considered him punished by God, stricken by him, and afflicted.

5 But he was pierced for our transgressions, he was crushed for our iniquities; the punishment that brought us peace was on him, and by his wounds we are healed.

NAHUM

NAHUM 1:9

Whatever they plot against the Lord he will bring to an end; trouble will not come a second time.

JEREMIAH

JEREMIAH 1:12

The Lord said to me, "You have seen correctly, for I am watching to see that my word is fulfilled."

JEREMIAH 30:17

But I will restore you to health and heal your wounds,' declares the Lord, 'because you are called an outcast, Zion for whom no one cares.'

JOEL

JOEL 3:10

Beat your plowshares into swords and your pruning hooks into spears. Let the weakling say, "I am strong!"

HEALING SCRIPTURES FROM THE NEW TESTAMENT

MATTHEW

MATTHEW 4:23-24

23 Jesus went throughout Galilee, teaching in their synagogues, proclaiming the good news of the kingdom, and healing every disease and sickness among the people.

24 News about him spread all over Syria, and people brought to him all who were ill with various diseases, those suffering severe pain, the demon-possessed, those having seizures, and the paralyzed; and he healed them.

MATTHEW 8:2

A man with leprosy came and knelt before him and said, "Lord, if you are willing, you can make me clean."

MATTHEW 8:16-17

16 When evening came, many who were demon-possessed were brought to him, and he drove out the spirits with a word and healed all the sick.

17 This was to fulfill what was spoken through the prophet Isaiah: "He took up our infirmities and bore our diseases."

MATTHEW 9:35-36

35 Jesus went through all the towns and villages, teaching in their synagogues, proclaiming the good news of the kingdom and healing every disease and sickness.

36 When he saw the crowds, he had compassion on them, because they were harassed and helpless, like sheep without a shepherd.

MATTHEW 10:1

1 Jesus called his twelve disciples to him and gave them authority to drive out impure spirits and to heal every disease and sickness.

MATTHEW 12:14-15

14 But the Pharisees went out and plotted how they might kill Jesus.

15 Aware of this, Jesus withdrew from that place. A large crowd followed him, and he healed all who were ill.

MATTHEW 14:14

When Jesus landed and saw a large crowd, he had compassion on them and healed their sick.

MATTHEW 14:35-36

35 And when the men of that place recognized Jesus, they sent word to all the surrounding country. People brought all their sick to him

36 ...and begged him to let the sick just touch the edge of his cloak, and all who touched it were healed.

MATTHEW 18:18-19

18 "Truly I tell you, whatever you bind on earth will be bound in heaven, and whatever you loose on earth will be loosed in heaven.

19 "Again, truly I tell you that if two of you on earth agree about anything they ask for, it will be done for them by my Father in heaven.

MATTHEW 21:21

Jesus replied, "Truly I tell you, if you have faith and do not doubt, not only can you do what was done to the fig tree, but also you can say to this mountain, 'Go, throw yourself into the sea,' and it will be done.

MARK

MARK 9:23

"If you can'?" said Jesus. "Everything is possible for one who believes."

MARK 10:27

Jesus looked at them and said, "With man this is impossible, but not with God; all things are possible with God."

MARK 11:22-24

22 "Have faith in God," Jesus answered.

23 "Truly I tell you, if anyone says to this mountain, 'Go, throw yourself into the sea,' and does not doubt in their heart but believes that what they say will happen, it will be done for them.

24 Therefore I tell you, whatever you ask for in prayer, believe that you have received it, and it will be yours.

MARK 16:14-18

14 Later Jesus appeared to the Eleven as they were eating; he rebuked them for their lack of faith and their stubborn refusal to believe those who had seen him after he had risen.

15 He said to them, "Go into all the world and preach the gospel to all creation.

16 Whoever believes and is baptized will be saved, but whoever does not believe will be condemned.

17 And these signs will accompany those who believe: In my name they will drive out demons; they will speak in new tongues;

18 ...they will pick up snakes with their hands; and when they drink deadly poison, it will not hurt them at all; they will place their hands on sick people, and they will get well."

LUKE

LUKE 6:17-19

17 He went down with them and stood on a level place. A large crowd of his disciples was there and a great number of people from all over Judea, from Jerusalem, and from the coastal region around Tyre and Sidon,

18 who had come to hear him and to be healed of their diseases. Those troubled by impure spirits were cured,

19 and the people all tried to touch him, because power was coming from him and healing them all.

JOHN

JOHN 10:10

The thief comes only to steal and kill and destroy; I have come that they may have life, and have it to the full.

ACTS

ACTS 10:38

how God anointed Jesus of Nazareth with the Holy Spirit and power, and how he went around doing good and healing all who were under the power of the devil, because God was with him.

ROMANS

ROMANS 4:16-21

16 Therefore, the promise comes by faith, so that it may be by grace and may be guaranteed to all Abraham's offspring— not only to those who are of the law but also to those who have the faith of Abraham. He is the father of us all.

17 As it is written: "I have made you a father of many nations." He is our father in the sight of God, in whom he believed—the God who gives life to the dead and calls into being things that were not.

18 Against all hope, Abraham in hope believed and so became the father of many nations, just as it had been said to him, "So shall your offspring be."

19 Without weakening in his faith, he faced the fact that his body was as good as dead—since he was about a hundred years old—and that Sarah's womb was also dead.

20 Yet he did not waver through unbelief regarding the promise of God, but was strengthened in his faith and gave glory to God,

21…being fully persuaded that God had power to do what he had promised.

ROMANS 8:2

2…because through Christ Jesus the law of the Spirit who gives life has set you free from the law of sin and death.

ROMANS 8:11

11 And if the Spirit of him who raised Jesus from the dead is living in you, he who raised Christ from the dead will also give life to your mortal bodies because of his Spirit who lives in you.

GALATIANS

GALATIANS 3:13-14

13 Christ redeemed us from the curse of the law by becoming a curse for us, for it is written: "Cursed is everyone who is hung on a pole."

14 He redeemed us in order that the blessing given to Abraham might come to the Gentiles through Christ Jesus, so that by faith we might receive the promise of the Spirit.

GALATIANS 3:29

29 If you belong to Christ, then you are Abraham's seed, and heirs according to the promise.

EPHESIANS

EPHESIANS 6:10-17

10 Finally, be strong in the Lord and in his mighty power.

11 Put on the full armor of God, so that you can take your stand against the devil's schemes.

12 For our struggle is not against flesh and blood, but against the rulers, against the authorities, against the powers of this dark world and against the spiritual forces of evil in the heavenly realms.

13 Therefore put on the full armor of God, so that when the day of evil comes, you may be able to stand your ground, and after you have done everything, to stand.

14 Stand firm then, with the belt of truth buckled around your waist, with the breastplate of righteousness in place,

15 and with your feet fitted with the readiness that comes from the gospel of peace.

16 In addition to all this, take up the shield of faith, with which you can extinguish all the flaming arrows of the evil one.

17 Take the helmet of salvation and the sword of the Spirit, which is the word of God.

2 CORINTHIANS

2 CORINTHIANS 4:18

18 So we fix our eyes not on what is seen, but on what is unseen, since what is seen is temporary, but what is unseen is eternal.

2 CORINTHIANS 10:3-5

3 For though we live in the world, we do not wage war as the world does.

4 The weapons we fight with are not the weapons of the world. On the contrary, they have divine power to demolish strongholds.

5 We demolish arguments and every pretension that sets itself up against the knowledge of God, and we take captive every thought to make it obedient to Christ.

PHILIPPIANS

PHILIPPIANS 1:6

6 ...being confident of this, that he who began a good work in you will carry it on to completion until the day of Christ Jesus.

PHILIPPIANS 2:10-11

10 that at the name of Jesus every knee should bow, in heaven and on earth and under the earth,

11 and every tongue acknowledge that Jesus Christ is Lord, to the glory of God the Father.

PHILIPPIANS 4:6-7

6 Do not be anxious about anything, but in every situation, by prayer and petition, with thanksgiving, present your requests to God.

7 And the peace of God, which transcends all understanding, will guard your hearts and your minds in Christ Jesus.

2 TIMOTHY

2 TIMOTHY 1:7

7 For the Spirit God gave us does not make us timid, but gives us power, love and self-discipline.

HEBREWS

HEBREWS 10:23

23 Let us hold unswervingly to the hope we profess, for he who promised is faithful.

HEBREWS 10:35-36

35 So do not throw away your confidence; it will be richly rewarded.

36 You need to persevere so that when you have done the will of God, you will receive what he has promised.

HEBREWS 11:11

11 And by faith even Sarah, who was past childbearing age, was enabled to bear children because she considered him faithful who had made the promise.

HEBREWS 13:8

8 Jesus Christ is the same yesterday and today and forever.

JAMES

James 5:14-15

14 Is anyone among you sick? Let them call the elders of the church to pray over them and anoint them with oil in the name of the Lord.

15 And the prayer offered in faith will make the sick person well; the Lord will raise them up. If they have sinned, they will be forgiven.

1 PETER

1 PETER 2:24

"He himself bore our sins" in his body on the cross, so that we might die to sins and live for righteousness; "by his wounds you have been healed."

1 JOHN

1 JOHN 3:21-22

21 Dear friends, if our hearts do not condemn us, we have confidence before God

22 and receive from him anything we ask, because we keep his commands and do what pleases him.

1 JOHN 5:14-15

14 This is the confidence we have in approaching God: that if we ask anything according to his will, he hears us.

15 And if we know that he hears us—whatever we ask—we know that we have what we asked of him.

3 JOHN

3 JOHN 1:2

2 Dear friend, I pray that you may enjoy good health and that all may go well with you, even as your soul is getting along well.

REVELATION

REVELATION 12:11

11 They triumphed over him by the blood of the Lamb and by the word of their testimony; they did not love their lives so much as to shrink from death.

HEALING THROUGH COMMUNION

We now believe communion is not merely a ritual to be observed, but it also a supernatural healing to be received. It's a blessing that should be received often, not just once a month in a church setting. Contrary to the way many believers were taught, no one that has fallen in sin should run away from the blood of Jesus (the cup), and no one sick should avoid eating his body (the bread). I believe that in times of sickness, it should be taken more often.

Nonbelievers can't rightfully expect God's favor. But, why are believers, who have a powerful blood covenant with God, weak, sick, and dying prematurely? The one biblical reason given for this is because they didn't "discern the Lord's body." ["For this cause, many are weak sick among you and many sleep...not discerning the Lord's body." 1 Cor. 11:29-30 KJV] In other words, while fully grasping the power of the blood to wash away all sins, we failed to equally grasp the power of Jesus' body to heal our diseases. In prayer, I heard the Lord say, "I know they don't 'discern' my body because they are not taking it with the same vigor with which they take other medications for healing."

Communion is a two-part blessing. When we take it, we remember that his blood washed away all our sins. In like fashion, we are reminded that his body was cruelly lashed and bruised with stripes and wounds for our total physical healing. It was equally just as much God's will to heal our bodies as it was to save our souls. The blessing is two parts, His blood washed away our sins. His body took away all our diseases.

The Psalmist wrote, "Forget not all His benefits. Who forgives all our sins, who heals all our diseases"(Ps. 103:3).

Even in our judicial system, when charges are dropped, the jailed person is physically set free. So it was in the

Supreme Court of heaven. When the charges against us were all cleared by Jesus' sacrifice, even the bodies of the saints which had died were released. Those saints were freed from their graves, and they showed themselves alive. Wow, what awesome healing power! (Matt. 27:52-53)

Supernatural health for the children of God doesn't only come from eating the right foods. It also comes from eating the body of Jesus, the Lamb of God, in communion. After 400 years of slavery the children of Israel were instructed to strike the blood of an innocent lamb over the side posts and doorposts. And God said, "when I see the blood I will pass over you." Once the blood was shed the people were instructed to eat the body of the Lamb.

When they did, they were physically released from bondage in Egypt and infused with supernatural health. The Bible describes that among the millions, "there was not one feeble among them." Likewise, today when we eat the body of the Lamb, remembering Jesus' death and resurrection, we receive that same supernatural healing.

In the beginning, it was what Adam and Eve ate that plunged them under the curse. Contrariwise, communion is something every believer can eat that will bring healing into his/her body. So let us do as Jesus instructed his disciples at the last supper, he said, "Take, eat, this is my body broken for you...this is the New Testament in my blood...drink it." Jesus said as often as you partake of communion you demonstrate my death. The astounding feature of his death was that his body was resurrected. Whenever you partake in Holy Communion, you take His body, by faith, and feed it into yours, taking on all His attributes. Jesus is essentially saying, "If your body is sick or weak, here, by faith, take mine."

www.ingramcontent.com/pod-product-compliance
Lightning Source LLC
Chambersburg PA
CBHW020430010526
44118CB00010B/513